THE AUTHENTIC LEADER AS SERVANT (ALS)

ALS II COURSE 7
NAVIGATION LEADERSHIP
Attributes, Principles, and Practices

SYLVANUS N. WOSU, Ph.D

THE AUTHENTIC LEADER AS SERVANT
ALS II COURSE 7
Developing Navigation Leadership Attributes, Principles, and Practices

© Copyright 2024 by Sylvanus N. Wosu Ph.D.

Printed in the United States of America
ISBN: 978-1-960224-34-7

All rights reserved. No part of this book may be reproduced or transmitted in any form or by any means, electronic or mechanical, including photocopying, recording, or by any information storage and retrieval system, without permission in writing from the copyright owner.

Bible quotations are from the New King James (NKJV) version of the Bible unless otherwise indicated.

Other versions used in this book are the New International Version (NIV), New Living Translation (NLT), King James Version (KJV), English Standard Version (ESV), and Good News Translation (GNT). Unless otherwise specified, NKJV should be assumed.

The views expressed in this work are solely those of the author and do not necessarily reflect the views of the publisher, and the publisher disclaims any responsibility for them.

To order additional copies of this book, contact:
Proisle Publishing Services LLC
39-67 58th Street, 1st floor
Woodside, NY 11377, USA
Phone: (+1 646-480-0129)
info@proislepublishing.com

PROISLE PUBLISHING

TABLE OF CONTENTS

FOREWORD — IX
ACKNOWLEDGMENTS — XIII
DEDICATION — XV
PREFACE — 17
    About Leader As Servant Leadership (LSL) Model — 20
    About the Authentic Leader as Servant (ALS) — 23
    About the ALS Courses — 24

CHAPTER 1
UNDERSTANDING LEADERSHIP ATTRIBUTES — 33
    Functional Definitions — 33
    Comparisons With Other Works — 38
    Principle of Leadership Attribute — 40
    Authentic Leadership Attributes — 41
    Summary 1 Understanding Leadership Process — 46

CHAPTER 2
NAVIGATION LEADERSHIP ATTRIBUTE — 49
    Characteristics of Navigation Attribute — 50
    Principle of Leadership Navigation Attribute — 51

CHAPTER 3
DEVELOPING THE NAVIGATION PREPARATION — 53
    Summary 3 Developing the Navigation Preparation — 55

CHAPTER 4
DEVELOPING THE NAVIGATION CHART — 59
    Summary 4 Developing the Navigation Chart — 60

CHAPTER 5
DEVELOPING THE NAVIGATION FOCUS ON DETAIL — 61
    Summary 5 Developing the Navigation Focus on Details — 64

CHAPTER 6
DEVELOPING NAVIGATION FOR ARRIVAL — 67
    Summary 6 Developing Navigation for Arrival — 72

TOPIC INDEX — 75
REFERENCES — 77

Foreword

The modern world today is obsessed with standardization and modalities. As a result, in the realm of leadership, many books have spout associated leadership theories and models and explain them as the path to follow. However, the critical dimensions that distinguish the effectiveness of any leadership process are the values and attribute the leader brings to the table; desired change is influenced by leadership styles or standards. These many standards and theories of leadership often are not in step with the changing times or the followers' needs. The trend is a bit like stocking different kinds of foods in a grocery store and expecting that they will meet everybody's needs the same way and at all times. Aisles are packed with varieties of food with expiration dates in the future, but getting the best deal on the products is what really matters to those who buy and use the products

In many ways, this is the state of leadership in the modern world. Increasingly, even leaders of public institutions are tasked with turning a profit for themselves or the organization they serve. The idea of a "leader" seems to float uneasily alongside the ranks of fundraisers or profit raisers in contrast to any kind of role model for followers or employees. That which is knowable, measurable, and marketable has surpassed the difficult intangibility of strong moral leadership attributes as the central guideline for achievement and success.

In this complicated space, Dr. Sylvanus Wosu introduces his complex idea of the Leader as a Servant Leadership, which is in this book, modeled on Christian tradition. Like all intricate ideas, Dr. Wosu's central point depends on a paradox: a person is best qualified to lead when he or she is most ready to serve. This paradox has been monopolized rhetorically by "public servants" who often serve either self-interest or the interests of specific lobbies. The Authentic Leader as Servant penetrates past the superficial concept of "serving" and details the internal state of true servitude or Servanthood.

While the book is primarily focused on the Christian model of leadership attributes such as discipleship, empathy, affection, and Servanthood, it does so not merely on the grounds of blind faith, but rather via numerous contemporary sociological and business-driven studies on how leaders should seek a leader-follower relationship that is simultaneously productive and nurturing. Dr. Wosu's most piercing insights always involve this secular–Christian dialogue. This book demonstrates that Christ's model for leadership is one that may exist successfully outside the confines of a faith relationship; it places the values of Christ's religious significance in leadership at the center of the framework. It is clear from Dr. Wosu's generous own life story of faith—a faith tested by humbling difficulties—is at the center of both his orientation and motivation for writing.

In language that is so concise, it is often illustrated in mathematical formulas; Dr. Wosu explains the deep structural integrity of Christ's Leader as the Servant Leadership model. One could imagine leaders of any doctrine benefiting from the analyses contained in these pages. The book's message repeatedly encourages the reader to imagine a scenario or reflect on memories and personal experiences to prove or test its many points. Thus, the book depends on a form of praxis, a lesson that could be or has been enacted, by the participating reader. I am very impressed at the volume and level of thinking of the author. Parts of the book involve his personal story, which is especially riveting. I cannot imagine what he had to endure, which he referred to as a" wilderness walk," to accomplish the goal he set for himself. His life stories on these pages are inspiring and stimulating.

In this way, the text eschews dogmatism in favor of the self-discovery Socratic Method of teaching and learning. The reader is not badgered into complying with a religious objective but is rather asked to consider the applicability of difficult biblical concepts in relation to modern life. It is a fascinating and very thought-provoking read.

Hence, the book does not seek to make the leader a servant, a cookie-cutter corporate buzzword, but rather asks the reader to imagine him or herself interacting with a range of concepts. One of Dr. Wosu's great strengths is his reservation when it comes to forcing his reading's interpretation on the material he presents.

The book parallels Biblical and modern leadership scenarios in ways that consistently provoke thought, and while it is clear Dr. Wosu has his particular leadership style; the space for the reader's own thoughts is always left open.

The book could not have been written in any other way with integrity. Its format and formulas are offered to the reader of the leader as a servant role that it analyzes in its pages. To find a text that instructs from this humble position is profoundly refreshing in a genre that is often packaged inside a cover with a sizeable picture of the "modest" author, smiling egotistically beneath a name spelled out in large, gold lettering. Throughout its pages, this text feels as if it serves the reader.

In the end, this is the most satisfying aspect of the book. There is no standardized approach to achieving successful leadership. There is no promise of power and a bigger payday; in fact, the book often proffers just the opposite. The reader is not encouraged to devalue the experience of leadership by finding some economic metric for marking success but is rather asked to think deeply about the most basic elements of internal and social interaction within the framework of a Christian tradition. What this means will be different for every reader. Indeed, even in the context of single chapters, I found myself questioning or re-evaluating moments of my own life. This book serves; it doesn't feel like filling in multiple-choice questions, staring at a wall of flavorless grocery products, or hearing the endless servant promises of today's political scene. It feels like a humble invitation to consider a single paradoxical element of a profoundly productive tradition.

-Tobias Bates

ACKNOWLEDGMENTS

A book on leadership attributes as aspects of Servant Leadership sprouted from the wealth of knowledge and the inspirations of many other leaders. Their writings were sources of inspiration, challenges, and examples of excellence to emulate. I acknowledge the leaders listed below for their help in one way or the other. I am very grateful and I hereby express my appreciation and thanks:

Mr. Wayne Holt, introduced me first to the subject of Servanthood in one of our Stephen Ministerial Training classes, and he is the one who has conducted his life as a leader–servant; he encouraged me throughout my writing;

Dr. Harvey Borovetz, Distinguished Professor and Chair of the Bioengineering Department, is a leader-servant in many ways, he modeled Servanthood and encouragement attributes throughout his leadership in an academic setting.

Dr. Clifford and Dr. Patience Obih, in so many measures exemplified the practical leadership attributes discussed in this book.

Pastor Lance Lecocq, Lead Pastor of Monroeville Assembly of God, for his excellent model of servanthood, empowerment, and emulation attributes to the ministerial team, I am thankful for his motivation and encouragement throughout the several hours on this project;

To my administrative assistant, Ms. Terri Cook, who was always the first to review the manuscript; I am very grateful for her dedication.

To the African Christian Fellowship USA, institutions, and all other organizations where I have served in one leadership capacity or the other, thank you for affording me senior leadership positions that provided the leadership platform and opportunities to grow as a leader.

Dr. Lawrence Owoputi, a brother I am proud to call my friend; for his dedication to serving others, his generosity, healing care, and responsibility attributes during our term in office and in chapter leadership positions; he taught me that excellent following is also part of good leadership;

To Tobias Bates, for his editorial work on the original draft of the book, and his dedication to completing the work.

Mr. Edward F. Kondis, a member of our Engineering Board of Visitors, for his always encouraging and moral support;

Dr. Enefaa N. Wosu, my wife and life partner, for her love, commitment, and prayer support, especially during those long night hours I was not there for her and her constant reminder of who I must be as a leader-servant. Without her support, forbearance, wisdom, and encouragement, this project would not have been completed; I say, thank you very much.

And to God alone be all the glory and honor for the divine inspiration and guidance in initiating and completing this life-transforming book project.

Dedication

I humbly submit this book back unto the gracious hands of God who inspired the writings through His Holy Spirit!

I dedicate this book to my virtuous wife of 45 years, Rev. (Dr.) Enefaa Wosu whose spiritual leadership is an important gateway to our home, and to our four wonderful children—Prof. Eliada Wosu-Griffin EL, HeCareth, Tamuno-Emi, and Chidinma. From them all, I learnt what it meant to be a leader-servant. I could not be blessed with better teachers.

PREFACE

What characteristics did Biblical leaders like the Apostle Paul, Moses, Joshua, and Nehemiah as servants of their people display outwardly that distinguished them from other leaders, both then and now? The Apostle Paul kept his focus to *emulate* Christ and endured all the infirmities and persecutions he suffered to complete his goal to preach the gospel of Jesus Christ. He inspired Timothy and others through his effective *discipleship* leadership to imitate him as he emulated Christ. Moses' outward display of his *trus*t in God's power earned him a good level of trust from the people and empowered him for the mission of delivery of God's children from bondage in Egypt; he had to *reproduce* himself in Joshua to complete the mission. But the greatest of them was Jesus Christ, who humbly sacrificed His life to finish the work of redemption. In His *Servanthood*, commitment, and love for the people, He became the ultimate *model* of a leader as a servant to *emulate*.

Let's consider for a moment secular leaders in these current times! For example, think of Henry Ford, who founded the successful Ford Motor Company; Bill Gates who created the global empire that is Microsoft; Albert Einstein, who in many ways is synonymous with a genius for his contributions to modern physics; Abraham Lincoln, remembered as one of the greatest presidents and leaders of United States; and many others like these we cannot mention. What did all these leaders have in common? What propelled them to turn their initial failures or challenges into eventual successes? None had a direct mentor or inherited any fortune from their parents. Nevertheless, they all eventually succeeded. These people can be distinguished from others based on their self-will to succeed, their self-confidence and belief in themselves, their self-determination, and their perseverance, among other characteristics. The distinguishing characteristics displayed externally in service or relationships toward others are the outward functional attributes that define that leader.

Think about yourself as a student, faculty member, or that new executive. What was it that made your journey to success different and even great? Students and colleagues, when they see or hear about my display of what I have referred to as the 'wilderness walk of faith', have asked me to share the critical attitudinal elements that made me remain inwardly resilient and undaunted and yet outwardly joyful in the difficulties I had faced. This book is the result of those reflections. Let me explain one such teaching moment.

Many years ago, sitting in my research lab on a Saturday morning trying to finish writing my dissertation, a fellow graduate student walked into the room to talk with me. He was contemplating terminating his graduate studies. He was a privileged single male student but felt the load was just too much.

"Sylvanus," he asked, with seriousness in his eyes, "your research advisor suggested that I should ask you, 'what is it that makes you tick?'.'What is it about you that makes you joyful and at peace with yourself and determined to finish, no matter the situations and high expectations we face in this department?"

What he asked me were deeply reflective questions, but I was willing and excited to answer them. Even so, before I do, let's look at the context. At that period in my life, I had four little children as a graduate student; in fact, more children than any of the faculties at that time, except for one faculty member who had eight children. I received little or no support from the department. I was then an international alien, did not qualify for financial aid, and was not given any research assistant position. I was, therefore, self-supported with two off-campus part-time jobs. I joked at being a minority of minorities, the only student in the department with such a label,—but I was self-willed to succeed. My adaptability attribute, coupled with perseverance and resilience, was all that I needed to succeed despite the odds against me. In every exam, homework assignment, or project I had to compete with students with full financial aid, plus they had nothing to distract their attention from their studies. I lived with the attitude that using disadvantages as an excuse was not an option. Aspiring to earn my Ph.D. was a life dream, and I was willing to give my ultimate best to actualize that dream even in the face of challenges. The choice was mine!

So I looked at my classmate and all I could see was a student striding through a valley through which I also walked. He needed me to show him how to walk the walk, to empathize with him. To answer his question, I smiled, not that I wanted to, but because it was just who I was. The joy he attributed to me was an overflow of my appreciation of God's grace that His life in me was externally manifesting His light to bless someone else. It was a great teaching moment; I capitalized on it to tell my classmate that my joy was not about me. He could see physically but about He who was in me, he could not see in the flesh; I needed him to know that I was just showing forth His life in me. At first, my classmate did not understand the spiritual prose or metaphor I was using. He looked surprised but open to hearing more.

I did not ask if he was a Christian. However, right on my desk was my small green pocket Bible. I opened to 2 Corinthians 12:9 (NIV) and handed it to him to read. As he read the passage: "But he said to me, 'My grace is sufficient for you, for my power is made perfect in weakness.' Therefore, I will boast all the more gladly about my weaknesses, so that Christ's power may rest on me," I noticed how absorbed he was in the words

He looked astonished and read it again, this time silently. "This is interesting, but what does this mean?" He asked. I took his question to mean, "How does this relate to my question?

I explained to my friend that the external attitudes he or my advisors saw in me that warranted the question, "What makes you tick" were inspired by my inner value system based on my faith in this same Christ and His teachings. My desire to manifest His life and self-confidence is all because of what He has promised in His word if I believed. I have believed His words and have gained self-determination and faith to make the right choices through Him for my life, and his spirit has given me perseverance and resilience to focus on finishing strong in pursuit of any goal. "With that faith, I have continued, more passionately and excitedly; I can look at my challenges and vulnerabilities and delight joyfully in them, even as an alien minority of minorities! His grace and power have empowered me to do all things I want to do. That is what makes me tick," I explained.

He looked at me as if he got his answer. "Wow, thanks!" he said, looking inspired and ready to face his challenges. As we concluded with a prayer, and he stood up to leave, I pointed empathetically to his face and said, "If I made it despite my challenges, you have absolutely no excuse but to persevere to complete your studies; you can make it too!"

It is fitting to report that this encounter with my classmate transformed his will and determination to continue. Yes, he was encouraged and went on to complete his graduate studies. He emulated self-will and perseverance from the example of the most vulnerable of all students in the department.

The inner value system of a Leader-Servant is founded not only on his faith but his self-will, coupled with self-leadership; it is the greatest mentor who can turn any situation into an inconceivable success. Self-will is the primary driver for determination, resilience, and perseverance. It is what wakes you up in the morning to ask for strength to do whatever it is you are setting out to do. Based on my life walk of faith, I can state with absolute certainty that faith is the unseen assuredness that can empower you to turn your life's probable impossibilities into great and improbable possibilities.

ABOUT LEADER AS SERVANT LEADERSHIP (LSL) MODEL

Looking at the testimony above, do you know the source that energizes the characteristics you display outside and how your inner self is related to what others see outside? What distinguishes you from others is what combines to define your attributes! As a follower, can you identify the characteristics that distinguish your leaders? As an executive, how do you base your evaluation of yourself? Or how do you evaluate that brand-new manager or new youth director you want to hire? To what do you compare the individual's qualities when you look at his CV? What is the basis of your measure? Do you know if you are a substantial leader? These personal questions and much more are the subjects of this two-volume book, 'The Authentic Leader as Servant Part I: The Outward Leadership Attributes, Principles, and Practices', is written in two parts; the second part 'The Leader as Servant Leadership Model. Part II'; deals with the Inner Strength Leadership Attributes, Principles, and Practices.

When we think about today's corporate greed, deepening divide between the haves and have-not, gridlock in political systems, conflicts and wars, high divorce rates, and the rich young ruler in the Bible, it is easy to agree that all these people share a few things in common: self-centeredness, pride, lack of compassion, and greed. There is a great need in today's suffering world for leader-servants who display leadership attributes. These attributes should be oriented toward selfless service to others. Indeed, our world is increasingly drifting away from global serving reality toward the self and apathy. The most credible message or model for a possible solution to this dilemma and the answer to several complex leadership questions can be found in the foundation of the ultimate leader-servant, Jesus Christ. This book defines the Leader as Servant Leadership attribute as the combined acts of two or more distinctive functional leadership characteristics exhibited in service and relationship toward others. There is no better time than now for a book that presents comprehensive and irrevocable facts and principles regarding how to develop effective attributes of the leader-servant.

The Leader as Servant Leadership Model
My first book on this subject, The Leader as Servant Leadership Model, explains that Jesus' servant leadership model is based on the notion of a Leader as a Servant and not on a Servant as Leader. There are four distinct differences between a Servant as Leader (Servant-leader) and the Leader as Servant (leader--servant) models. It is pertinent to highlight them here to connect to this book, Authentic Leader as Servant.

A Leader as Servant is a leader first. The leader–servant as a leader does not in the line of duty go projecting or lording his or her power and authority over others but is the person to lead the process of influencing desired changes in others through his humble example of being a servant or having a serviceable attitude toward others. He or she is a serving leader, not a lording leader. He leads as a servant by putting others' needs above his own needs and rights. Jesus emphasized the word "as" meaning that the leader (the Master) chooses to serve as a servant even though he is the leader. A leader–servant emulates Jesus, who gave up all rights, and emptied and expended Himself on His followers. He empowered them to become more like Him. A leader-servant is known as a leader first but is seen as a great leader by his humble attendant heart and acts of service to others. His greatness comes from his ability to put others above himself.

Leader as Servant is a Biblical Concept. The model or image of a humble serving leader motivated Jesus' disciples to see that if their master could do this for them, they must also be able to do it for others. Jesus clearly demonstrated the process of leader-as-servant leadership. In some cases, He chose to serve by leading when He wanted to create the image or model of the leader-servant in certain acts. In other cases, He chose to lead by serving, when he showed care and empathy toward the people and led the disciples to see empathy as a leadership attribute.

Leader as Servant is an Authentic Leadership Model to follow. The Leader as the Servant leadership model intentionally positions Jesus as an original model of a leader to follow.

He was serving His disciples to demonstrate that the process of becoming a great leader was earned through humble acts of service to others; He made them understand that He was empowering them to succeed Him as leader-servants through service to others. The result was an incomparable legacy of leadership that changed their communities. The fact that Jesus relinquished his rights or shared His power did not diminish His power and influence. In fact, his influence increased at least 11 X 100%, if we ignore the one case of Judas.

The Leader as Servant Transforms Organizational Culture. The proposed LSL model seeks to transform and sustain the community or organization by instilling key leadership values or "leadership presence" among followers or an organization's members. Change is sustained when everyone in the organization takes ownership of the change. Rather than focusing on leading more followers to be great followers who conform to the organizational culture, LSL seeks to lead and empower better leaders to be distinguished leaders and community builders.

There are four distinctions, which clearly differentiate many of the existing servants as Leader-based philosophies in relation to servant leadership from my LSL model. Even in the corporate or institutional worlds, there is nothing better than Jesus on which to base Servant Leadership. There is nothing more authentic and impacting than the servant leadership modeled by the life and teachings of Jesus Christ.

The LSL model uses exploratory questions, scenarios, and graphic visualizations to excite critical thinking in ways no other book on this subject has yet attempted. Several personal testimonies of my wilderness walk of faith with God are used to connect the reader to real-life experiences of the concepts discussed. The riveting effect is that the text engages and encourages the reader to walk through the experiences presented. The aim is to inspire the reader spiritually, mentally, and professionally with this far-reaching exposition on the subject of servant leadership.

ABOUT THE AUTHENTIC LEADER AS SERVANT (ALS)

The *Authentic Leader as Servant* argues that no leadership model is as authentic, other-centered, able to build communities, and productive and service-oriented as the model of our ultimate leader-servant, Jesus Christ. No source can provide a better point of reference than that provided in the Bible. Hence, this book aims to be more than just a text on leadership; it hopes to be a personal discovery for those who aspire to develop effective leadership attributes that grow leaders as servants who ultimately develop thriving other-centered communities. This book presents a comprehensive, biblically-based study regarding how to develop these attributes and how they are applied in a servant leadership process. In this biblical context and for clarity, Servant Leadership means *Leader-as-Servant Leadership*. A *leader-servant* refers to a *leader as a servant*, which is distinct from a servant-leader or servant as leader.

Leader as Servant Leadership attributes are shaped by the Leadership's Inner Value system, which consists of character, motivation, and commitment. The *Authentic Leader as Servant* is presented as a necessary resource to complement my *The Leader as Servant Leadership (LSL) Model*. The LSL model integrates a transformative leadership framework and interactive dimensions of Servant Leadership. Leader as Servant Leadership is a process in which a leader, in his leadership position, purposefully chooses to put others' rights and needs above his positional rights and personal needs. He then serves, enables, and empowers followers for growth that builds a thriving organization. The LSL model looks at the predominant Servant Leadership concepts and shares how they compare with biblical principles on how we should lead and be led.

ABOUT THE ALS COURSES

The three books, *LSL Model* and *The Authentic Leader as Servant* (Parts I and II), together demonstrate that with today's global visions to reach people of all races and cultures, now is the time for an authentic servant's heart of service. Those visions and the leadership processes are most effective with the appropriate leadership attributes centered more on people than on the organization, principles regarding how to develop effective attributes of leader-servant.

The ALS I and II combined presented twenty leaders as servant leadership attributes. The series of ALS courses supply training guide to understand, develop, and practice the attributes in a leadership process. Each course is independent and self-contained and does not depend on completing any other course in the series of 20 courses. It is, however strongly recommended, in fact a must read, that chapters 1 and 2 in each series be covered as they lay the foundation of LSL model on which ALS is based.

ALS (Parts I & II) Course Layout

The *Authentic Leader as Servant (ALS)* leadership (parts I and II) book has been broken down into 20 courses in workbook format to achieve three goals 1) Self-discovery of the acts of developing the attribute under review in the course, 2) deeper understanding of the principles, research and biblical teaching behind the attributes, and 3) Learning the strategies for practicing the attributes.

Instruction

The set of questions following each chapter are designed to serve as a guide to discover, explore, and practice the essential ALS leadership attributes, principles, and practices in leadership process. The questions are comprehensive review based on the content of this specific chapter only.

To maximize the learning outcomes, the learner must read through this chapter and sections. Some referenced scriptures in the book are repeated in the summaries for added review if needed, even though they were discussed in the section in which they apply.

> The exercises that follow each chapter will help you in not only understanding your own strength and weaknesses in your acts of the attribute but will guide you in developing practical strategies you can apply in self-leadership process or helping others grow in leadership
>
> All answers to the questions are contained in the associated chapter or sections; consultation of new sources, except for the reference scriptures, is not needed. Thus, it is expected that you answer the questions after you have read the associated section or chapter of the workbook. The scripture or other references cited are only for references as they already discussed in the book

---

ALS II Course 1: Adaptability Leadership Attribute—*Flexibility overcomes rigidity in new and changing situations.*

Adaptability is framed as an inner strength quality of a leader in responding to changing needs or situations in a service mission. According to the Army training Handbook, adaptability is "an individual's ability to recognize changes in the environment, identify the critical elements of the new situation, and trigger changes accordingly to meet new requirements." God showed Moses adaptability when he empowered him to use the rod in his hand as an instrument for the mission ahead of him. This course will attempt to give meanings to personal reflective questions to discover the distinguishing characteristics of Leadership Adaptability. Numerous techniques, personal examples, empirical case studies, and applications of the adaptability developing strategies are discussed concepts. Practice questions at the end of each chapter are used to guide your development and to frame meanings out of the content to improve your acts of adaptability in a leadership process.

ALS II Course 2: Courage Leadership Attribute—*Courage is the inner strength of the mind to triumph over paralyzing fears of purposeful action that yields good success*

Courage Leadership Attribute is the lynchpin of effective Servant Leadership that supports the display of all the other attributes? Having the inner strength of character and convictions to persevere and hold on to new and often misunderstood ideas in the face of opposition takes courage—inner strength to triumph over the fear of failure or danger. It is even greater courage to venture into positions or overcome situations that nobody like you, has gone to before or where many better qualified than you had gone and failed. In all cases, they all display courage in the face of obstacles and uncertainties. The success is more about courage than the experience. Can such courage be learned or inspired? How do leaders or successful people in their callings get to their heights of achievements? How can courage be an inner strength within or beyond leadership? How does courage attribute triumph over paralyzing fear? This course explores answers to these questions and more by searching for the distinguishing characteristics of courage. Numerous techniques, personal examples, empirical case studies, including practice questions at the end of each chapter are used to guide your development and to frame meanings out of the content to improve your acts of courage leadership process.

ALS II Course 3: Empathy Leadership Attribute—*A measure of a leader's compassion is the empathic engagement in a follower's experience and state of well-being beyond just expressions of feelings and concerns.*

Empathy attribute is the ability to project one's personality and experiences into another person's thoughts, emotions, direct experience, position, and act toward the wellness of that person. How can a leader walk along with someone in that individual's "wilderness" state of suffering or danger? What motivates a leader to *empathize* with a follower? How is empathy an inner strength leadership attribute? Whether it's in your church, your business, your institution, or in your community, this course provides a comprehensive biblical-based discussion on the role of a leader as a servant in empathizing with those he leads. The aim is to inspire the reader spiritually, mentally, and professionally with this far-reaching exposition on empathy in servant leadership. How can a leader make a lasting positive impact in the lives of those he or she leads? Answers to these and other personal reflective questions are explored in this course on Leadership Empathy Attributes. Numerous techniques, personal examples, empirical case studies, including practice questions at the end of each chapter are used to guide your development and to frame meanings out of the content to improve your acts of empathy leadership process.

ALS II Course 4: Encouragement Leadership Attribute—*The direct measures of encouragement are the inspired strength and quality of uplifted spirit to persevere toward a desired outcome.*

There are times when people want to grow in their potential, want to change their present situation, feel emotionally low in lived experiences, or feel as if they should be appreciated for a job well done. In any of these cases, some encouragement goes a long way to lift up the spirit of someone low. A case study is of the leadership qualities of Barnabas, named the "Son of Encouragement" by the disciples (Acts 4:36), because they saw him as an *encourager*. You can only be an encourager from the strength of your inner personality. The act of encouragement is mostly expressed or *given* to inspire growth or apply a spiritual gift to serve others. What did the disciples see in Barnabas? Obviously, he must have affected them with his acts of encouragement. They saw him as an encourager by his *courage* to *inspire* them at a time they desperately needed to move the ministry forward. This course explores the distinguishing characteristics of encouragement attributes in servant leadership. Each characteristic of encouragement attribute will be discussed in detail with emphasis on strategies of how they can be further developed or practiced by a leader-servant in a leadership process. Practice questions at the end of each chapter are used to guide your development and to frame meanings out of the content to improve your acts of encouragement leadership process.

ALS II Course 5: Initiation Leadership Attribute—*Initiation creates the catalyst for a vision, and the vision when acted upon, produces a desired change.*

The initiation of a process for a desired change is the core of the inner strength of a decisive leader in any leadership process. Initiation leadership is the act of taking step to originate or get something started. In general, initiative is an "individual's action that begins a process, often done without direct managerial influence." The primary outcome of the initiation attribute is that it leads to desired change; something new in the lives of the followers or organization, such as a new growth in followers, a new product or policy in an organization, or a new mission or mission agenda. How do leaders take action to begin a process of change? What are the distinguishing initiation characteristics of leaders such as Moses and Nehemiah in working according to God's agenda? How does a leader conceive a strategic vision for initiation action?. or negotiate his way to influence possible actions toward that vision. This course explores answers to these, and other questions based on examples from Nehemiah (Nehemiah 1:4 through 2:6-8) and Moses and God (Exodus 3 and 4:1-14).

ALS II Course 6: Listening Communication Leadership Attribute
—*Effective communication occurs at the convergence of listening attention, hearing, and understanding of the information transmitted.*

A leader-servant face three important types of communication at one point or the other. At the core is listening ability as the inner strength and ability to receive and understand the meanings of words and messages internally and accurately in a two-way communication process. How does a leader-servant communication with God, the Holy Spirit, and followers (individually or collectively) to be most effective. The course explores how the three elements—words spoken, unspoken, and in the spirit—offer unique reflections of the communication process and what they share in common. How does listening serve as a critical element of effective communication between people forms the bridge by which a leader can be effective?. A leader's capacity to listen to communicate effectively depends on the leader's inner strength to perceive, hear, and understand the information from written, verbal, and non-verbal exchanges. Each characteristic of listening communications attribute will be discussed in detail with emphasis on strategies of how they can be further developed or practiced by a leader-servant. Practice questions at the end of each chapter are used to guide your development and to frame meanings out of the content to improve your acts of listening leadership process.

ALS II Course 7: Navigation Leadership Attribute—*Leaders who prepare for and chart through a purposeful course of action arrive with their followers at the desired destination.*

The navigation attribute is having a *vision* for the intended destination plus the direction to get there. Having a vision is a quality of the inner strength of a leader and the path that the leader follows in the life journey is often influenced by internal and external factors. The organizational culture and climate collectively combine to make an organization unique through the diversity of employees' characteristics, values, needs, attitudes, and expectations. How does a leader-servant *navigate* and *negotiate* his actions through the organization and people he serves, individually or collectively, to *finish* or *arrive* at his purpose? How do you prepare your followers to *finish* strong or *arrive* at their destinations? This course explores answers to these and other questions and how a leader's inner strength capacity can empower him to navigate the cultural bridges to influence the desired change in others in their personal and professional needs and attitudes.

ALS II Course 8: Responsibility Leadership Attribute—L*eadership responsibility is the measure of the quality of a Leader's accountability for the growth of followers and the organization*

Responsibility leadership refers to possessing the capability and accountability needed in the act of being responsible (trustworthy, dependable, honest, etc.) in a leadership process. At a personal level, it defines the level of your position (pastor, deacon, department head, janitor, etc.) in your church, family, or employment. Responsible leaders in their positions *choose* to emphasize the positive, uplifting, and flourishing side of organizational life. Are there qualities in your position that need to be trained or developed to influence positive outcomes in people and organizations? Organizationally, what are the attributes of the leadership structure, process, and culture that are most conducive for maximizing the growth of followers and organizations in service toward others? How can responsibility qualities be developed to enhance high-quality relationships, emotional competencies, positive communication, beneficial energy development, and positive climates for the effective leader as a servant leadership process? The course explores answers to these and other questions. Distinguishing leadership characteristics of responsibility attributes are identified and discussed in detail. Practice questions at the end of each chapter are used to guide your development and to frame meanings out of the content to improve your acts of responsibility leadership process.

ALS II Course 9: Stewardship Leadership Attribute—*A measure of good stewardship is the entrustments' better and richer growth change at the end than at the beginning*

ALS Navigation Leadership
Attributes, Principles, & Practices

*Stewardship leadership is the process of u*tilizing and managing the resources entrusted to you by someone. We recognize that God has ownership of everything above, and below the earth. In that context, we are all stewards of what God owns, including our lives but entrusted to us to be managed and maintained in a purposeful manner that will honor God. What are the distinctive servant leadership characteristics of stewardship and how can they be developed? This course explores answers to these questions with reference to servant leadership. Practice questions at the end of each chapter are used to guide your development and to frame meanings out of the content to improve your acts of steward leadership process

ALS II Course 10: Vision Leadership Attribute—*You have a vision when you understand how you get to your mission-purpose and what the future outcome will be relative to your present.*

The vision leadership attribute gives the leader the ability to specify in the present *what* each follower's or group's growth should be in the future, *where* to focus these efforts to meet that growth; *how* he will accomplish all aspects of his mission, *which* future (destination) he aspires to lead the people, and *when* the purpose will be achieved. Leadership without direction leads followers to nowhere. Vision is the most common descriptor of effective leadership and must be clear and inspirational in order to achieve desired purpose. What are the qualities a visionary leader? When was the last time you added brand new challenges to your normal routine to achieve a new you? Answers to these and other questions are explored in this course. The primary characteristics of visionary leadership will be identified and used to frame a principle of leadership vision attribute. Practice questions at the end of each chapter are used to guide your development and to frame meanings out of the content to improve your acts of encouragement leadership process.

Referenced Scriptures

A variety of Bible translations from over 11,200 original Hebrew, Aramaic, and Greek words to about 6,000 English words do exist with variations in meanings and emphases. I am not a biblical scholar and do not pretend to be one; Hence, I have avoided researching the roots of these words and personally prefer New King James Version (NKJV). I have intentionally used other translations for three main reasons; first, to allow for increased impact and alignment of words to the most desired meaning and emphasis in the concepts being addressed. Second, I wanted new and personal discovery of meanings from translations with which I have not been familiar. And third, I wanted to allow readers who may desire translations other than the NKJV the benefit of their preferred translations. Hence, in addition to the NKJV, other translations used in the book include New International Version (NIV), New Living Translation (NLT), King James Version (KJV), English Standard Version (ESV), and Good News Translation (GNT). Unless otherwise specified, NKJV should be assumed.

Sylvanus Nwakanma Wosu

CHAPTER 1
UNDERSTANDING LEADERSHIP ATTRIBUTES

Leadership attribute is the combined acts of two or more distinctive functional leadership characteristics exhibited in service and relationship toward others.

The starting point of our discussion is the understanding of the key functional definitions and concepts that describe the theme of this book. In general, 1 will define leadership as an integrative process in which a person applies appropriate attributes to guide and influence the sought-after attitudinal changes in others toward accomplishing a particular goal. Specifically, the Leader as Servant Leadership is a process in which a leader intentionally chooses to put the follower's rights and needs above his positional rights and personal needs, and serves, enables, and empowers them for desired spiritual and professional growth that builds thriving communities.

FUNCTIONAL DEFINITIONS

In the context of these definitions, I will begin the descriptions of the leadership attributes of an authentic leader-servant by offering a functional definition of Leadership Attributes, and showing how that definition differs from those of Leadership Character, Characteristics, and Traits.

Leadership Character is the sum total of personal qualities in leadership, such as honesty, values, vision, trust, and so on that make up the moral capital of the leader; Leadership character should describe who the leader is inside or the leader's basic personality traits.

The Leadership Characteristics describe the distinctive characteristics or features of a leader, such as attitudes, competencies, skills, and specific experiences that go beyond his character (personality). Leadership characteristics determine how (through skills and competencies) the leader leads or take actions in the process of leadership in any particular situation;

The Leadership traits are the distinguishing leadership characteristics of a leader (these are things that define his leadership characteristics), which differentiate from personality traits... Leadership traits are the set of characteristics that define a particular leader's leadership. This means that a leadership characteristic is a trait when it is a unique characteristic of the leader.

Leadership Attributes, unlike leadership character, characteristics, and traits, is *a leadership attribute and the combined act of two or more distinctive functional leadership characteristics exhibited in service and relationship toward others* or traits externally displayed in action toward others. All leadership attributes grow out of the leadership inner value system but can be externally displayed predominantly as an outbound or outward attribute or both:

1. **Outbound Attributes:** These are distinctive outward-bound attributes emanating from the inner strength of the leader to support external conduct in service and relationships toward others. They form the internal core functional qualities that motivate or enhance the outward manifestation of the inside character toward others. The outbound attribute such as listening and vision, for example, are the direct results of the inner values of the leader such as patience, hearing, love, humility, or all the fruits of the spirit.

2. **Outward Attributes:** These are distinctive functional outward outer visible attributes emanating from the richness of the outbound and inner values of the leader. For example, external attributes such as Servanthood, emulation/modeling, empathy, etc. are outflows from the leader who will directly impact the follower. Outward attributes can be enriched by the outbound (inner) attributes. As shown in Figure 1, the outward attributes in general form the outer core of

functional attributes in the leader as servant leadership, but they can share some overlapping functions with the outbound attributes.

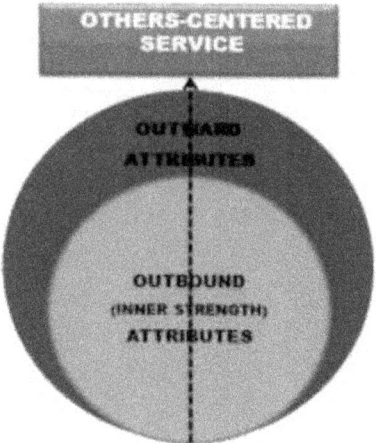

Figure 1.1. Servant leadership functional attributes

In summary, a leadership attribute is more than an ability or a characteristic; it is making those characteristics or abilities functional as part of how the leader acts (his habits) in service to others and applying those characteristics (beyond just having them) in personal and service relations to others. The character or known characteristic defines some aspects of your abilities or who you are inside— e.g. honest, humble, brave, etc. Your attribute, on the other hand, defines your habits; a display of how you use your characteristics, or the actions you exhibit toward others because of who you are inside. For example, empathy as a leadership characteristic becomes a leadership attribute if the followers can distinguish the leader's acts or habits of empathy, such as walking through with his followers in their state of suffering to bring wholeness; otherwise, it is just a characteristic or ability. Leadership attributes toward others are what impact the followers' and the organizational growth more than ability and competence.

In addressing one of the self-righteous hypocritical attributes of servitude leadership, Jesus called leader-servants to be "inside-out" leaders that reflect credibility; indeed, leaders should not appear outwardly righteous when they are full of hypocrisy and lawlessness in their hearts. He was describing "inside–out" as an authentic leadership attribute measured by the display of credibility a leadership attribute!

ALS NAVIGATION LEADERSHIP
ATTRIBUTES, PRINCIPLES, & PRACTICES

The measuring stick of a leader-servant is Jesus Christ. We measure ourselves unto the measure of the status of the fullness of Christ (Ephesians 4:13).

The leadership attributes of an authentic leader as a servant are encapsulated in **SERVANT/SERVING LEADERSHIP** are listed in Table 1.1, and defined in Table 1.2: *Servanthood, Emulation, Responsibility, Vision, Navigation, Adaptability, Trust, Listening, Empathy, Affection, Discipleship, Encouragement, Reproduction, Stewardship, Healing-Care, Initiation, Integrity,* and *Persuasion.* Other support attributes include *Influence, Courage, and Generosity.*

The attributes have been separated into Outward and Outbound (Inner Strength) leadership Attributes. As shown in Table 1.1, each of these attributes has three or more leadership characteristics. As such, more than 65 leadership characteristics are covered in these 20 attributes. For example, a leader's Servanthood leadership attribute is characterized by his willing servant's heart of selfless role humility, sacrifice, and submissiveness. The more these are present in a leader, the more effective the servant leadership.

Table 1.1: The functional leader-servant leadership Outbound (Inner Strength) and Outward attributes

	LEADER-SERVANT LEADERSHIP ATTRIBUTES			INNER STRENGTH ATTRIBUTES	OUTWARD ATTRIBUTES
S	Servanthood	L	Listening	Adaptability	Affection
E	Emulation	E	Empathy	Courage	Discipleship
R	Responsibility	A	Affection	Empathy	Emulation
V	Vision	D	Discipleship	Encouragement	Generosity
A	Adaptability	E	Encouragement	Initiation	Healing–Care
N	Navigation	R	Reproduction	Listening	Influence
T	Trust	S	Stewardship	Navigation	Persuasion
I	Influence	H	Healing–Care	Responsibility	Reproduction
G	Generosity	I	Initiation	Stewardship	Servanthood
C	Courage	P	Persuasion	Vision	Trust/Integrity

The list does not assume that a leader has to be excellent in all attributes or even have all of them to be an effective Leader–Servant. However, the more of these attributes the leader displays in his acts of service toward others, the more productive he or she will be, and the further his impact on the followers and organization. The table also shows that two or more attributes can share common characteristics, which can be applied or observed in different contexts. For example, a leader's ability to inspire followers can be seen in his acts of discipleship, empowerment, an.d encouragement attributes in the context in which these attributes apply. Each attribute is exhibited either as a part of the outbound inner strength attribute of a leader or a part of the outward attribute. Table 1.1 is not an exhaustive list of attributes; in fact, there are hundreds of such attributes. This is just the starting point.

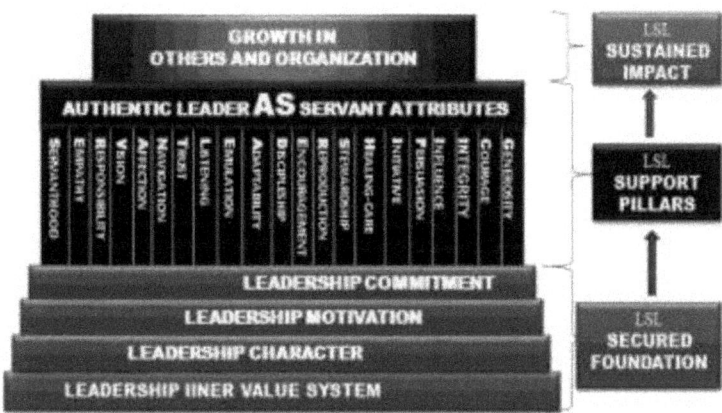

Figure 1.2: Servant leadership outward attributes (dark blue) and relationship to four foundational layers of the LSL Model

Figure 1.2 shows that the leader's attributes are shaped and secured by his four foundational layers (leadership inner value system, leadership character, motivation, and commitment). The attributes of the leader–servants are also conceptualized as the support pillars that will establish and support the personal authenticity of the leader, what the leader, does and the effectiveness of the leadership process. Thus, the attributes represent functional pillars of authentic leadership that can be learned or enriched as described in detail in the subsequent chapters. The combined effect of a secured foundation and stable support pillars will make a sustained impact on the growth of followers and the organization.

COMPARISONS WITH OTHER WORKS

The original works by Greenleaf (1970) in servant leadership [1] have been reviewed by Larry Spears (1996), who identified listening, empathy, healing, awareness, persuasion, conceptualization, foresight, stewardship, commitment to the growth of others, and building community as the ten distinguishing characteristics of servant leadership. [2] Russell (2001) has studied these attributes and have shown them to be essential in servant leadership and concluded that these qualities generally "grow out of the inner values and beliefs of individual leaders." [3] Russell and Stone (2002) extended the Greenleaf 10 attributes to 20 attributes observed in servant-leaders. These 20 attributes were categorized by these authors as either functional attributes (intrinsic characteristics of servant-leaders) or accompanying attributes (complement attributes that enhance the functional attributes).[4] The operational attributes were identified as vision, honesty, integrity, trust, modeling, service, pioneering, appreciation, and empowerment with the accompanying attributes of communication, credibility, competence, stewardship, visibility, influence, persuasion, listening, encouragement, teaching, and delegation. Only three of the attributes identified by Greenleaf were identified, and all three were accompanying attributes rather than functional. Responsibility, adaptability, affection, discipleship, navigation, and reproduction attributes which are considered critical in biblical-based servant leadership in my LSL model are not covered by Russell and Greenleaf. As shown in the description of the attributes in Table 1.2, most of the attributes reported by Russell and Stone (2002)[5] or Greenleaf [1] can be seen either in the twenty attributes or their associated characteristics. Integrity and honesty for example are leadership characteristics of trust and other attributes rather than an independent attributes. I take the position that servant leadership attributes are functional attributes in acts of duty to others and emanate from the inner value system of the leader.

Table 1.2: Description of the functional leader-servant outward leadership attributes and associated principles and characteristics

Leader–Servant Leadership Attributes	Principles of Leadership Attributes	Leadership Characteristics
Affection: This is the combined love-based works toward providing the essential help or services for the spiritual growth or survival of another person.. (Chapter 2)	Affection flows from a person to produce positive emotions for the well-being of another person	Kindness Compassion Practical Love Affective signs Appreciation
Discipleship: This is the combined acts of personally developing, intentionally equipping, and attentively empowering growth in others to reproduce a heart of service. (Chapter 3)	Discipleship transforms and empowers followers for service leadership that grows communities.	Inspiring Shepherding Equipping Developing Empowering
Emulation: This is the combined acts of initiating an authentic servant attitude as a model of service worthy of following (Chapter 4)	A great leader-servant outwardly and positively inspires a pattern of good works for others to follow.	Inspiration Motivation Initiation Model Following
Generosity: This is the combined acts of freely sharing with and giving to others as an act of kindness, without expectation of reward or return to him. (Chapter 5)	Generosity is an outward measure of the level of sacrifice, what is shared, or the impact a giving makes, not just the size of the giving.	Sharing Giving Kindness Affection Love
Healing-Care: This is the combined acts of providing comfort and empathy to make others whole emotionally and spiritually along with tending to the follower's physical and mental well-being. (Chapter 6)	Comforting others in any trouble with the comfort with which we are comforted by God, brings healing - wholeness.	Self-Healing Empathy Reconciliation Comfort Relational
Influence: This is the combined acts of positively affecting desired change in conduct,	The true measure of leadership success in affecting	Model Positive attitude Authority

ALS Navigation Leadership
Attributes, Principles, & Practices

performance, and relational connections toward others-centered course of action or service. (Chapter 7)	desired change in conduct, performance, and relational connections in others is influence	Connection Wisdom Intelligence,
Persuasion: This is the combined acts of communicating perspective to connect, challenge, and convince with a compelling purpose to convert others to a new position. (Chapter 8)	The means of transforming others to a new perspective is through empathetic persuasion	Connecting Challenging Communicating Convincing Converting Encouraging
Reproduction: This is the combined acts of developing your leadership qualities in others and releasing them as successors to continue a greater mission. (Chapter 9)	Great leaders produce successors for legacy and greater courses as an expected product of an effective leadership reproduction.	Selecting Mentoring Equipping Empowering Releasing
Servanthood: This is the combined acts of humility, willingness, and intentionality in service to others through selfless sacrifice and submission as a servant. (Chapter 10)	A leader-servant is most qualified to lead when most ready to serve as a servant for the growth of others. The role of a leader is to serve as a servant	Servant's heart Humility Sacrifice Service Willingness Submissiveness
Trust: This is the combined acts of positive display of character, competence, credibility, and shared relational connections that produce assured trust-confidence of the trustee in the trusted. (Chapter 11)	True leadership trust produces assured trustee's confidence and readiness to follow based on the credibility, competence, and shared relational connections of the trusted.	Character Competence Integrity Credibility Confidence

PRINCIPLE OF LEADERSHIP ATTRIBUTE

In the context of servant leadership, a leadership attribute is a level above the leadership characteristic or trait of a leader. The principle of leadership attribute states that every leadership attribute has a set of distinguishing characteristics that make up the inward or outward display of the attribute. The principle reflects the essential designed purpose or outcome of the attribute or the inevitable consequence of the effective practice of the attribute. Thus, the principle of leadership attribute is a concise statement about the fundamental truth, value, or belief about the attribute in a leadership situation; it is a statement that establishes an idea about the outcome of the attribute for guiding the practical application of the attribute and its characteristics. I will postulate and frame each principle as an additive function of the characteristics of the attribute. A statement of each principle is quoted at the beginning or below the title of each chapter. It is yet to be experimentally proven if the attribute is a linear or some other non-linear function of these characteristics as variables. It is expected, however, that each character will contribute to the effectiveness of the attribute in varying degrees.

AUTHENTIC LEADERSHIP ATTRIBUTES

At a personal level, attributes are the value-based inside-out moral leadership assets that can be related to the authenticity of a leader-servant. The complexity of defining authenticity has been noted in the literature. The subject of authentic leadership is well covered in the works of Terry (1993),[5] George (2003),[6] and Shair and Eilam (2005).[7] All appear to agree that authenticity requires self-awareness and objective self-identity in personal and social interactions with others. In his book, *Advocacy Leadership*, Professor Gary L. Anderson offers individual, organizational, and societal perspectives on authenticity: "Authenticity, at a peculiar level, is living a life, whether in the private or professional term. This is congruent with one's espoused values; at the structural level, authenticity has to do with viewing human beings as ends in themselves, rather than means to other ends; at the public level, it is a state of affairs that is congruous with the shared political and cultural values of society."[8]

The basic tenets of these perspectives are very fitting to authenticity as a qualifying element of leader-servant leadership attributes. The attribute reflects how the followers see the leader based on the leader's distinctive features displayed through his or her actions personally, organizationally, and societally. The leader is seen as a leader-servant or serving leader because the followers see him lead as a servant from an inside-out value of others. This is what makes the leader authentic.

Authenticity means that what a leader displays outside, in personal or leadership life of service to others, and society is based on the values the leader espouses inside.

Authenticity in servant leadership can be one or two types or both: *Outbound Authenticity and Outward Authenticity*. The Outbound (outward-bound) Authenticity is the genuineness of personal honesty from your inner strength and abilities; what you say and how you act emanate from who you are or how you feel inside. It reflects the essential truth and honesty about your outward-bound inner strength.

Outward authenticity, on the other hand, describes the truthfulness of your credibility and honesty displayed outward in relation to others; your *outer* visible behavior or how you act outwardly towards others reflects exactly your true intentions.

While *outward* authenticity is the visible *outer* indicator of the truth of who you are inside, *outbound* authenticity is outward-bound attribute from the inside of who you are. Credibility in this context is the influence a leader has to attract believability, trustworthiness, and authenticity; it is the believability, trustworthiness, and authenticity of who you are inside and outside.

A key element of personal authenticity is that it is seen or measured in the context of societal, cultural, and organizational interactions. In that context, achieving individual authenticity becomes a challenge since it is influenced by social factors and dispositions of individuals who usually depend on liberal and organizational realities. However, for leader-servant leadership, the leader can face those changing times by remaining focused on his key Biblical-based principles or *Leadership Inner Value System*. Thus, I am interested in authenticity as an essential element of effective Leader-servant leadership attributes or Leader-servant leadership attributes as drivers of leadership authenticity. With that in mind, the first critical element of authenticity in practicing or developing efficient leader-servant leadership attributes is inside-out self-examination relative to the people served rather than the organization. You may ask yourself: What will be my response when the people I lead act or react in a certain way, will it be negative or positive? What are my strengths and vulnerabilities at those times?

Professor Yacobi in his post, "Elements of Human Authenticity," noted that since "the self -arise attribute emerges from interactions between self, others, and the environment in a complex society and

CHAPTER 1
UNDERSTANDING LEADERSHIP ATTRIBUTES

world, there may co-exist multiple complicated identities depending on place and context." [9] He went on to identify the following <u>essential elements of personal authenticity</u>: self-awareness, unbiased self-examination, accurate self-knowledge, reflective judgment, personal responsibility, and integrity, genuineness, and humility, empathy for others, understanding of others, optimal utilization of feedback from others. All of these are covered under the leadership attributes or characteristics shown in Table 1.2.

Bill George, in his book, *Authentic Leadership*, takes the position that to be an authentic leader; a person must have the following essential characteristics: [10]

- Behavior based on value: He must understand his own values and exhibit behavior to others based on those values;
- He must not compromise his values in difficult situations but could use the situation to strengthen personal values in those situations.
- Passion from a clear purpose: Be self-aware of who he is, where he is going, and the right thing to do.
- Compassion from the heart: He must lead from a compassionate heart that allows them to be sensitive to the plight and needs of others,
- Connectedness from a relationship; he must be relationally connected with people he leads,
- Consistency from the self-disciple: He must demonstrate self-discipline to remain calm, collected, and consistent in a stressful situation.

Modeled after the elements above, Table 1.3 lists six essential characteristics of authenticity for servant leadership. These fundamental characteristics cover the five identified above and can also be aligned with the leadership characteristics in Table 1.2. Each attribute in Table 1.2 is expected to pass the personal authenticity test in Tables 1.3, 1.4. In a survey of 132 Christian leaders, seventy-four percent (74%) of them agreed that they always or frequently exhibit servant leadership attributes. [11] Thus, a pass of the outward authenticity test means that a pure leader must demonstrate 70% or more of these essential elements of this legitimacy. (That is, 70% YES in the assessment questions in Tables 1.3, 1.4).

It needs to be noted, however, that a secular leader could be authentic and still lack some of the essential servant leadership attributes or characteristics such as selflessness, servanthood, and love-motivated servant attitudes of a leader-servant. Effective leader-servants are authentic leaders and personal authenticity is an essential element of leader-servant leadership. The key test for leader-servant authenticity is the quality of his inside-out value and personal character. What is most important is a change from the inside-out.

Table 1.3: The test of essential elements of personal inner strength authenticity in servant leadership

	Elements of Inner Strength Authenticity	Inner Strength (Outbound) Authenticity Assessment Questions	YES / NO
1	Personal inside-out value-based behavior	Are your personal inside-out values aligned with acts of service and behavior outside?	1
		Are you honest to yourself in relation to your inner strengths and abilities?	2
2	Inside-out Self-Awareness	Do you have unbiased self-examination, and accurate self-knowledge of who you are inside-out?	3
		Do you know your inner strength and weaknesses in relation to the good you want to show as an outward attribute?	4
3	Inside-out Empathy-Compassion	Do you know and feel from your inside what you want for your followers?	5
		Are you motivated to empathize, based on your inside feelings?	6
4	Inside-out Connection with followers	Do you feel deep, personal, and spiritual connection with your followers?	7
		Does what you say and how you act reflect how you feel when you relate to others?	8
5	Inside-out Emotional Self-regulation	Do you have difficulty controlling your emotion in order to remain calm in a stressful situation?	9
		Are you always able to comfort yourself?	10
6	Inside-out Authenticity Feedback	Do your followers see your inside-out value from your outside behavior?	11
		Will your followers feel that what you say you are is congruent with how you act?	12
#YESs____; # NOs____: Outbound Authenticity: YES/ 12-----%			

CHAPTER 1
UNDERSTANDING LEADERSHIP ATTRIBUTES

Table 1.4: The test of essential elements of personal outward authenticity in servant leadership

	Elements of Personal Outward Authenticity	Personal Outward Authenticity Assessment Questions	YES or NO
1	Personal value-based outward behavior	Are your personal values and beliefs aligned with your acts of service and behavior toward others?	1
		Do you live out your life according to your beliefs?	2
2	Personal Self-Awareness	Do you have clarity of your personal vision and purpose?	3
		Does what you know about yourself accurately describe what others say?	4
3	Personal Outward Empathy-Compassion	Do you apply how you feel to what your followers need?	5
		Do you lead from a compassionate heart and are you sensitive to the plight and needs of others?	6
4	Personal Connection with followers	Do you feel deep, personal connection with your followers?	7
		Does your outward action toward others reflect exactly your true intentions?	8
5	Outward Emotional Self-regulation	Do you have difficulty controlling your emotions to remain calm in a stressful situation?	9
		Does your evaluation of your value of others agree with how valued they feel?	10
6	Personal Authenticity Feedback	Do your followers see your outward acts as true and honest?	11
		Can your followers see other-centeredness in 70% or more of your attributes?	12
#YESs____ ; # NOs____ : Outbound Authenticity: YES/ 12-----%			

ALS NAVIGATION LEADERSHIP
ATTRIBUTES, PRINCIPLES, & PRACTICES

SUMMARY 1
UNDERSTANDING LEADERSHIP PROCESS

Before starting this exercise, please read and follow the instruction in the preface of this workbook. Answers to these questions are contained in this chapter. Completion of these exercises after reading the chapter should take 60-90 minutes.

Discovering the Leadership Attributes

1. What is your alternative definition of leadership? In learning to lead, how would you differentiate the following elements:
    a. Leadership.
    b. Leader as servant leadership.
    c. Leadership characteristics.
    d. Leadership attributes.
2. What are the key differences between the Leader as Servant and the Servant as Leader Leadership philosophies?
3. What was the original source of the Servant as Leader (SL)? What was the original source of Leader as Servant (LS)?
4. What is the key framework of a Leader as a Servant Leadership?
5. Authenticity in servant leadership can be one or two types or both *Outbound Authenticity and Outward Authenticity*: Describe a time when you displayed:
    a. The Outbound (outward-bound)—*outbound* authenticity is outward-bound attribute from the inside of who you are.
    b. *The Outward Authenticity*—*outward* authenticity is the visible *outer* indicator of the truth of who you are inside,
6. Describe the key elements of personal authenticity seen or measured in the context of societal, cultural, and organizational interactions.
7. How are the essential characteristics of authentic leader in leadership process in challenging times?
8. How much of a leader-servant are you? Take the personal leader-servant audit in Table 1.5 to self-assess your effectiveness.
9. Based on the questions in Table 1.5, can you identify each of the twenty attributes? What ones did you score 3 ("sometimes") or less than 3? Review and learn and commit to work to improve.

CHAPTER 1
UNDERSTANDING LEADERSHIP ATTRIBUTES

Table 1.5. Leader As Servant-Leadership Audit

A servant-leader in his leadership position purposefully choses to serve and inspire acts of service in others by his example. Select and circle best answer to questions
1=Never; 2=Almost never; 3=Sometimes; 4=Frequently; 5 =Always

	Servant Leadership assessment questions	Circle no				
1	I am willing and other-centered, and readily chose to serve others as a servant for their personal growth	1	2	3	4	5
2	I model others-centered attitude in my service and relationships and inspire same for others to follow	1	2	3	4	5
3	I have a sense of obligation, willingness, and accountability for the service towards others	1	2	3	4	5
4	I have the foresightedness to specify in the present view what others' growth should be in a given future	1	2	3	4	5
5	I work toward providing the essential help or services for the spiritual growth or survival of the others;	1	2	3	4	5
6	I provide the needed purposeful course of action for how to chart the course to for my followers.	1	2	3	4	5
7	I display external credibility and a strong sense of character based on values, beliefs, and competence;	1	2	3	4	5
8	In communication, I attentively perceive and hear what is communicated, reflectively listen to understand and to be understood	1	2	3	4	5
9	I walk through with others in their state (suffering, emotions, etc.) in a way that provides the needed care and well-being	1	2	3	4	5
10	I have a measure of self-secured flexibility to adapt appropriate attitude to serve all people in different situations	1	2	3	4	5
11	I personally develop, intentionally equip, and attentively nurture spiritually growth in others	1	2	3	4	5
12	My act of bravery instills in others the courage and confidence to follow or persevere in a course of action	1	2	3	4	5
13	I develop my leadership qualities in others as successors to continue in a purposeful mission	1	2	3	4	5
14	I manage, maintain,, and account for all resources entrusted to me and being responsible for the difference my acts make	1	2	3	4	5
15	As a care-giver, I act to comfort and make others whole emotionally	1	2	3	4	5
16	When I see a need, I originate a vision and action, and stay committed to meet that need and desired change	1	2	3	4	5

ALS NAVIGATION LEADERSHIP
ATTRIBUTES, PRINCIPLES, & PRACTICES

17	I display a holistic view of an issue to inform, transform or convert others to my view through empathetic persuasion	1	2	3	4	5
18	I freely share what I have sacrificially as an act of kindness to others, without expectation of reward in return	1	2	3	4	5
19	My act of influence is to affect the actions, behavior, opinions, etc., of others based on trust, credibility and relationship	1	2	3	4	5
20	In the face challenges and danger, I act with bravery to overcome fear and take a stand with strength and conviction	1	2	3	4	5
Score Range	Add up the numbers in each column (Total Score____) Check and Understand the key areas to work on					
81-100	Strong Leader-Servant; keep it up, go and train others.					
66-80	Above average Leader-Servant; work 25% of key areas					
50-65	Average but developing; need to work on 50% of key areas					
34-49	Below average leader; work on 75% of key areas					
<34	Not a Leader-Servant; need training in all areas					

CHAPTER 2
NAVIGATION LEADERSHIP ATTRIBUTE

Leaders who prepare for and chart through a purposeful course of action arrive with their followers at the desired destination.

There are several paths toward which effective leaders in today's dynamic world will want to point their followers. The beginning of a great leader-servant is being competent and growing in his knowledge of Christ to lead others in the right path of fruit-bearing as Christ did. To be effective in this regard, a leader must first be fruitful and be willing to walk with others along in the challenges they may face to bear fruit. This fruit must include living a spirit-filled life. Helping others live that same life requires the leader's inner strength capacity to help navigate through a path of abundant life.

The path that one follows in that life journey is often influenced by internal and external factors. Leaders must be able to lead themselves internally through those factors such as challenges in organizational culture and climate, and regulating his emotions to lead others. Let us consider the following working definition: The culture of an organization with respect to servant leadership can be referred to as a shared system of inner values, beliefs, and expectations that sharp policies, perceptions, and attitudes of people in that organization. The environmental or internal climate of an organization is the dominant force for attitudes, habits, and behaviors of people toward others in that organization. These two definitions show that the culture of a place can affect its climate, and vice-versa, and how a leader leads. The organizational culture and climate collectively combine to make an **organization** unique through the diversity of employees' characteristics, values, needs, attitudes, and expectations... A leader's leadership effectiveness, therefore, depends to a large extent on his inner strength capacity to influence the desired change in the culture and climate in which he serves; he must guide the followers in navigating through the organization with their personal and professional needs and attitudes. The organizational culture and climate can affect the quality of life of the people and their levels of engagement and productivity. Because both the workplace and overall organization are defined by their cultural norms, a leader's navigation attribute helps him find his bearings in new organizational cultures and help to understand members of that culture better.

Take a moment and think about the culture and climate in which you work, serve, or lead. Are there some challenges that those situations present against the path you or your followers must walk in the journey to success? What could be some effective strategies to use to navigate through those challenges? In this chapter, we will explore answers to these and other questions. We will identify the distinguishing characteristics of navigation leadership attributes and come up with a functional definition, principle, and practices of navigation attributes.

CHARACTERISTICS OF NAVIGATION ATTRIBUTE

Successful global players use the Cultural Mapping and Navigation Program to manage intercultural dynamics. [14] Cultural Mapping is a tool for identifying the inter-cultural strength of a community and is also used to train leaders to develop their intercultural intelligence/competency and leadership ability. Cultural Mapping is implemented through a process of collecting, recording, and analyzing the cultural assets (strengths, interests, cultural values) of the organization. In Nehemiah's case, understanding the culture enabled him to provide a supportive climate of trust, teamwork, and a reward system to increase people's engagement.

CHAPTER 2
NAVIGATION LEADERSHIP ATTRIBUTE

A leader-servant *navigates* and *negotiates* his actions through the organization and people he serves, individually or collectively. Think of a time you dealt with a challenge that involved several people in your organization; a time you went on a mission trip to an unfamiliar place, or a time you made an important decision that required sharing power. How did you navigate the action (move or influence your idea) through the people, the system, and the culture, to *finish* or *arrive* at your purpose?

Navigation means having a *vision* for the intended destination plus the direction to get there, and having a vision is a quality of the inner strength of a leader. The critical first step in navigation is *preparation*. According to John C. Maxwell, "When you prepare well, you convey confidence and trust to the people....Leaders who are good navigators are capable of taking their people just about anywhere. [15] How do you prepare your followers for a task? Good *preparation* is followed by a *chart* or map that is produced using the information received during the preparation stage. The plan and the map chart the course about to where you are going, but you *finish* strong or *arrive* at your destination only if you can *focus* on the directions specified in the map.

PRINCIPLE OF LEADERSHIP NAVIGATION ATTRIBUTE

From the above review, the leadership navigation attribute is characterized by the leader's ability to *Prepare, Chart* the course, *Focus,* and *Finish* or *Arrive* at the destination. These characteristics lead me to the following definition:

> *Servant leadership navigation attribute: The combined acts of preparing for and charting a purposeful course of action, leads followers to a destined growth.*

The growth could be the arrival at a spiritual, professional, or physical goal plus leading the organization to accomplish its mission.

Servant leadership -Navigation-attribute is about charting toward a mission direction or taking an organization and followers through a course of action in a mission without drifting outside the vision direction. It is about charting through a journey for success. Here is the principle:

Servant leadership navigation principle: Leaders who prepare for and chart through a purposeful course of action arrive with their followers at the desired destination.

This principle is expressed by the following equation:

PREPARE + CHART + FOCUS + FINISH = NAVIGATION

If you have used today's global positioning system (GPS), you must have experienced the joy of arriving at the correct destination or the frustration of arriving at the wrong destination. I remember heading to a wedding with my wife and another couple in the car. I thought I had keyed in the correct address into the GPS and did not know I had incorrectly clicked the wrong address in the list of suggested destinations. The information we received earlier was that the trip to the wedding locale was less than 10 minutes from our hotel. With the wrong address in the GPS, however, a journey of 10 minutes took 30 minutes to the wrong destination and another 35 minutes back to the correct destination when the error was rectified. My initial poor preparation (not making sure of the correct address); a wrong chart (keying in the wrong address); even with a good focus on what I thought was correct, resulted in arriving at the wrong destination with everybody (followers) on board. Sadly, we did not finish well! The wedding was over by the time we changed courses and got to the correct address!

Servant Leadership Navigation Attribute is modeled as a four-stage process illustrated in Figure 8.1

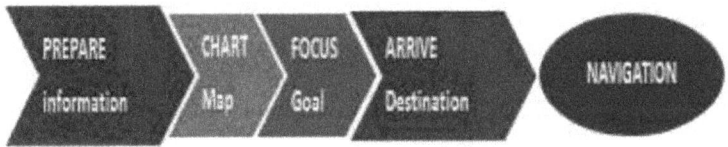

Figure 8.1. Servant leadership navigation attribute model

CHAPTER 3
DEVELOPING THE NAVIGATION PREPARATION

The navigation preparation stage is planning the roadmap and the starting point of the navigation process and involves building the framework for the plan, understanding what is at stake, and gathering correct information and all that is necessary to develop an effective course of action. Nehemiah in the face of his challenge to rebuild the broken wall of Jerusalem is a good example of how-to pre-plan a course of action in navigating through a situation. Before beginning the building process as a course of action, Nehemiah planned ahead as his first key element of navigation. His course of action featured a set of well-defined strategies:

Plan to use the correct information

Planning for action starts with having a view of where you are going and getting the necessary information to direct the course of action for the mission. The effectiveness of the action you take depends on the quality, completeness, and correctness of the information you have. Nehemiah spent time grasping the situation and was inspired to act based on what he understood. He made himself aware of the challenges, and the people's problem became his problem and his burden to bear. He personally took steps to assess and understand the situation fully; he knew how long the rebuilding would take, and the resources he needed.

What happened in the U.S./Iraq war following the 9-11 tragedy that took more than 3,000 lives is an example of a course of action based on incorrect information. The information leading to the action for the war was later shown to be outdated and poorly conceived. As a result, the reason for engaging in the war was based on incorrect and confusing information, which resulted in a misleading direction and wrong destination. A leader cannot reach a desired goal with poorly conceived direction and strategies.

Map out the course of action

Mapping out the course of action includes expecting and planning for the opposition. This may require investigating and understanding the thinking of the opposition and countering that plan. Nehemiah expected and prepared himself for any opposition that he might encounter. His next step in mapping out the plan after he understood the situation was prayer. He wanted to work according to God's agenda, not his. He spent time weighing the options and praying for wisdom for the right course to follow. His prayers deepened his ownership of a need and empowered him to take the first initiative to define the vision purpose and seek God's favor. When a leader hears from God, he does not want unwanted advice.

Understand the cultures to navigate

The leader must learn the language of the culture and should acquire culture-based communication skills to negotiate and find a middle ground if multiple cultures present an issue. Nehemiah understood the culture of his people, but he also had to learn to understand the culture of the community around him, which could influence the plan. One of the elements of business in today's global village is interacting and engaging people across cultures.

Engage the key people in influence

To navigate your way through a complex situation (that is usually bigger than you), you need support from others. You will also need to communicate with them the possible course of action. Nehemiah identified the key people of influence; he communicated his vision and course of action; he established clear and honest communication; and finally, he directly asked and received permission, resources, and support to rebuild. The Leader-servant's function is to guide or direct people or followers to understand the mission and to get buy-in. Nehemiah navigated his way through the hearts of the people to obtain buy-in for the final plan and integrated his interests into the interests of the people to carry out these functions.

Be prepared for sacrifice in the work

Nehemiah made serious sacrifices to move the project forward, even though the followers started falling behind in their commitment. He encouraged each person and prepared them for the sacrifice. He also encouraged them to be strong in the presence of any opposition, including, fighting and dying for the course of action. Jesus wanted his disciples to follow His plan, but they had to forsake all to follow him and the plan, even giving up their lives. Jesus also showed them that there is a greater reward for those who follow the plan to reach their destination.

SUMMARY 3
DEVELOPING THE NAVIGATION PREPARATION

Before starting this exercise, please read and follow the instruction in the preface of this workbook. Answers to these questions are contained in this chapter. Completion of these exercises after reading the chapter should take 60-90 minutes.

Discovering Navigation Leadership Attributes

1. There are several paths toward which a leader will want to point individuals and followers toward desired change. What does navigation-preparation stage mean?
2. What do you consider to be the critical steps before you begin your journey to a success destination?
3. Mapping out the course of action includes expecting and planning for uncertainties:
   a. How do you plan for such uncertainties?
   b. How can a leader be equipped to navigate such culture of uncertainties?
   c. How can the leader guide the individuals and followers collectively in navigating through the organization to meet desired change?

ALS NAVIGATION LEADERSHIP
ATTRIBUTES, PRINCIPLES, & PRACTICES

Practicing the Acts of Navigation Leadership Attribute

1. Think about the culture and climate in which you work, serve, and lead or a community in which the culture needs to change to accommodate the growth of all, especially the marginalized individuals in it:
   a. List some challenges that those situations present against the path you must walk in the journey to success?
   b. What could be some effective strategies to use to navigate through those challenges?
   c. What are some distinguishing characteristics of the navigation leadership attribute?
2. **Navigation-preparation for road -map** defines the starting point of the navigation process and involves:
   a. What are some key elements of the Navigation-preparation?
   b. How can a leader build the framework for the plan?
   c. What are the four key actions in setting well-defined navigation preparation strategies?
      a. How many acts of the navigation as an attribute do you display?
      b. Take the leadership navigation Attribute audit in Table A. 1
      c. What navigation qualities did you score < 3 and how can you improve in those areas?
3. With reference to navigation leadership attribute, what take-away, meaning or lesson can you frame to improve your acts of navigation leadership attribute in a leadership process? Write a commitment statement for plan to improve.

Chapter 3
Developing the Navigation Preparation

	Table A. 1. Leadership Navigation Attribute Audit					
	Servant leadership navigation attribute is combined acts of preparing for and charting a purposeful course of action that leads to a destined growth. Assess the quality of your acts of navigation by inserting an X below the number that best describes your response to each statement.					
Item	**Acts of Navigation Attribute Check** **1= Always; 2= Frequently; 3= Sometimes;** **4: Almost Never; 5= Never**	1	2	3	4	5
1	I know the starting point in my leadership navigation road-map					
2	I engage the key people of influence					
3	I am able to build the framework for the plan for action with key specifics					
4	My course of action is based on specific details from my preparation					
5	I am usually prepared and willing to make the needed sacrifice for the work					
6	I arrive at purposeful goal through influencing a unified vision of the chart for action					
7	As the driver behind navigation wheel, I am able to concentrate on the details of the plan with the end goal in view.					
8	I do watch out for distracters in my navigation focus					
9	I have a positive destination-attitude and usually to complete the mission-goal as expected					
10	I maintain persistent resilience toward the destination					
	Add up your rating in each column					
Score Range	Guide and Explanation of Score: understand the areas you need to further develop;	Total Score =				
10-17	Great Navigator; keep it up!					
18-25	Above Average; need to work on 25% of the areas					
26-33	Average navigator; need to work on 50% of the areas					
34-41	Below average- work on 75% of the areas					
42-50	Not a Navigator ; need to work on all the areas					

CHAPTER 4
DEVELOPING THE
NAVIGATION CHART

A Navigation chart is the blueprint of the course of action with all the specific details based on the preparation stage of the process. A true measure of successful navigation to arrive at a destination as a unit—without drifting from the mission—is influencing others to have a unified vision of the chart for action:

Create a unified vision of the chart

Nehemiah met with the people and cast the vision for them. In doing so, he built the needed synergy for rebuilding and encouraged the people to develop buy-in. He also educated the people on why the course of action was imperative; indeed, their distress was over Jerusalem lying at waste. He personally committed himself to oversee the project. He also showed them the consequences if they did not take action. The situation was a reproach to Israel and with the ruined wall and burned-down defenses, no one was protected. He created vision and passion in them by assuring them that God's hand was on them, presenting the plan with passion and confidence that worked in his favor. Ultimately, the King gave him permission to come and rebuild. Nehemiah encouraged and inspired others into action to accomplish God's will, and they all followed; "Then they said, 'Let us rise up and rebuild.' 'Then they set their hands to this god work" (Nehemiah 2:18, NKJV).

Align action with the mission-purpose

Effective leaders do not change the plan in the middle of a preplanned course of action. There is a need for decisiveness and conviction not to allow distractions and compromises that deviate from the plan. When leaders change course, their compromises of values and convictions jeopardize the mission. Every plan requires the leader to balance his faith in God and prepare for the mission (Joshua

8:1-29) and for God's divine guidance to make the plan effective. As a leader, Joshua laid a good plan and warned followers about the rough road ahead. He maintained the right perspective and foresight (was farsighted) as he executed the plan. In addition, when following the plan, the leader must think of exit options if things go wrong and include a damage prevention plan.

SUMMARY 4
DEVELOPING THE NAVIGATION CHART

Before starting this exercise, please read and follow the instruction in the preface of this workbook. Answers to these questions are contained in this chapter. Completion of these exercises after reading the chapter should take 60-90 minutes.

Discovering the Acts of Navigation-Chart

1. How is a navigation chart   the blueprint of the course of based on the preparation stage of the process.
2. A true measure of successful navigation to arrive at a destination as a unit is influencing others to have a unified vision of the chart for action.
3. From the perspective of Nehemiah, how can the following strategies increase leaders' ability to influence other:
    a. Create a unified vision of the char(Nehemiah 2:18, NKJV).
    b. Align action with the mission-purpose (Joshua 8:1-29)

Practicing the Acts of Navigation-Chart

1. **The navigation chart for action** is the blueprint of the course of action with all the specific details based on the navigation-preparation process.
    a. What is the true measure of successful navigation?
    b. What are three ways you can chart for an action?
2. With reference to navigation leadership attribute, what take-away, meaning or lesson can you frame to improve your acts of navigation-charting in a leadership process?
3. Write a commitment statement for plan to improve.

CHAPTER 5
DEVELOPING THE NAVIGATION FOCUS ON DETAIL

Think again about the global positioning system (GPS) in today's modern vehicles or in many phones, where you simply input the direction, you are going, and the system leads the way. The system directs all your turns and guides you to your destination. However, you will miss your mark, at least with current limitations, if you fail at any step to focus on the details of the road—stop signs, bridges, traffic lights, and pedestrians crossing the road.

This is also the way leader-servants such as Moses, Joshua, Nehemiah, and others walked with God. These leaders depended on the GPS directed by the Spirit of God and were careful to follow God's agenda. Not following God's agenda was a risk they did not want to take. The navigation focus is the stage in which the leader as the driver concentrates on the details of the chart with the end goal in view. We learned this in the life of Moses, who failed to reach his destined Promised Land because he failed to submit completely to God's directions.

He failed to focus on what mattered most: Moses' failure in navigation. Moses' desired destination was the Promised Land with the children of Israel. However, he must chart the course of action in three phases and must be successful in all. First, he must go to the Pharaoh and deliver them out of bondage from Egypt. Second, he must lead them through the desert. Third, he must lead and enter the Promised Land with them; that was his destination. Moses failed in his journey to success because he lost focus on God's ways. Throughout most of the journey, Moses judiciously followed God's map and directions in the first two phases of the mission. Nevertheless, toward the end, in the third phase, Moses shifted focus, disobeyed and mistrusted God at the waters of Meribah-Kadesh where he struck the rock twice with his rod when God had expressly told him to speak to it to produce the needed water (Numbers 20:8-11). The reason Moses struck the rock twice can be debated, but the record points to one possible reason: God had allowed him to strike the rock in Horeb for water (Exodus 17:6) but this time in Meribah (Numbers 20:3-14); He wanted him to speak to the rock for a specific reason—to be honored before Israel. Out of anger, Moses lost the perspective of God's ways and could not see the difference between the rocks at Horeb and Meribah-Kadesh and the honor that was of value to God. If Moses had kept God's ways in focus and self-regulated his emotions, he would have just done as God instructed as he had done before. Rather, he shifted focus to himself and abused the power God gave to him.

In the end, Moses did not reach the intended destination and failed in the navigation principle: He was prepared for the journey, but his one act of disobedience was not purposeful in God's eyes and for that reason, he failed to arrive at his followers at the desired destination. Without focus, leaders lose perspective of what is eternal value to God.

Be decisive and focused on your direction

Not drifting away from the direction is to be decisive regarding where you're going, keeping your eyes open. One moment of losing attention in our GPS example will set you driving on the wrong road. That was the case with Moses. Hence, as the leader/driver, you must be attentively decisive about where you are going and know and accept the truth of the next turn. We must choose to continue in a course of action even in the presence of opposition. When problems arose in executing his plan, Nehemiah was faced with difficulties. Still, he remained focused on the plan by motivating and listening to the people and having open communication to assess and adjust the plan where necessary. In the case of Moses, he reacted wrongly and failed. We must be prepared to face the challenges the course of action presents. We must have an instinctive feeling that failure is not an option and must be so determined and focused on reaching the destination that we must choose to ignore all distractions.

Watch for distracters

Even when the plan has been made and the initial buy-in accomplished, when implementing the plan, there will always be potential distracters, opposition, ridicule, resistance, false rumors, negative attitudes, and fear. The antidote to these distractions is a commitment to remaining focused. Nehemiah experienced all of these distractors and responded to each by relying on God. He respected the opinion of the opposition without compromising his beliefs; he reassured his people that they had God with them; and he continually reenergized the people. For example, when he sensed fear in the people, he encouraged them, "Don't be afraid of them. Remember the Lord, who is great and awesome, and fight for your families, your sons and your daughters, your wives, and your homes" (Nehemiah 4:14, NJKV).

Watch the front and back of the mission.

As Nelson Mandela celebrated his 90th birthday, Richard Stengel interviewed him and summarized his eight lessons of leadership [13]

1. Courage is not the absence of fear; it is inspiring others to move behind it.
2. Lead from the front but do not leave followers behind
3. Lead from behind and let followers feel they are in front.
4. Know your enemy and learn about his favorite spots
5. Keep your friends closer and your rivals even closer
6. Appearance matters and always remember to smell good
7. Nothing is black and white
8. Quitting is leading

The first three of these lessons are critical elements of the navigation attribute of leader-servants. Jesus also exemplified these three paradoxical principles. He was a leader yet a servant; He was God yet a humble man. He was in front and yet empowered them to follow his example. Most of when Jesus was physically present with the disciples, he was in front but made them feel as part of Him. One servant leadership quality exemplified by Nehemiah was that he remained very close with the people-friends and foes and was involved hands-on through the process.

After Jesus' death and resurrection, he led his disciples from within and behind through the Holy Spirit guiding and protecting them. He led from behind and let the followers feel they were in front when he gave power away to the 70 to empower them to serve others

(Luke 11:1-24). Both the 12 and 70 multiplied Jesus' impact. He was not physically present with them, but he was spiritually present for "Lo, I am with you even unto the end of the earth" (Matthew 28:20, KJV). They were leading, but Jesus was behind them. He spent a lot of time praying for the success of His inner circle (John 17:1-26). The lesson here is that, if you want to be great, you have to serve; that is, you have to take the lower and humble position. Being behind does not make a leader less than he is. Rather, it is a process of developing others to lead.

SUMMARY 5
DEVELOPING THE NAVIGATION FOCUS ON DETAILS

Before starting this exercise, please read and follow the instruction in the preface of this workbook. Answers to these questions are contained in this chapter. Completion of these exercises after reading the chapter should take 60-90 minutes.

Discovering the Acts o Navigation-Focus

1. Think about leaders like Moses, Joshua, Nehemiah, and others walked with God. These leaders depended on the "GPS" directed by the Spirit of God and were careful to follow God's agenda.
   a. Define the elements of the navigation-focus..
   b. What happens when a leader fails to follow the correct GPS instruction?
   c. Why and how did Moses fail to reach his destined Promised Land? (Numbers 20:3-14);
2. How can a leader be decisive and focused on his direction
3. What is the direct impact of distracters in following your "GPS" and how can you avoid or deal with it

Practicing the Acts of Navigation-Focus

1. **Navigation-focus on details** is the stage where the leader as the driver concentrates on the details of the chart with the end goal in view.
   a. What are the strategies for the navigation focus?
   b. How do watch out for distracters in the navigation focus?

CHAPTER 5
DEVELOPING THE NAVIGATION FOCUS ON DETAIL

2. As Nelson Mandela celebrated his 90th birthday, some lessons of leadership were learned from him. Fill in the blanks:
   a. _____ is not the absence of fear; it is inspiring others to move behind it.
   b. Lead from the _____ but do not leave _____ behind
   c. Lead from _____ and let _____ feel they are in front.
   d. Keep your friends _____ and your _____s even closer
   e. Nothing is _____ and _____e
3. As with Mandela, how did Jesus exemplify the paradoxical principles of leader-servant leadership? (See Luke 11:1-24; Matthew 28:20; John 17:1-26).
   a. Leader yet a servant;
   b. God yet Man,
   c. Want greatness, the serve,
   d. In front yet followers behind empowered
4. With reference to navigation leadership attribute, what take-away, meaning or lesson can you frame to improve your acts of navigation-focus in a leadership process?
5. Write a commitment statement for plan to improve.

CHAPTER 6
DEVELOPING NAVIGATION FOR ARRIVAL

Continuing our analogy to GPS, finishing well is to hear the GPS announce your arrival: "You have arrived; your destination is on the left." The leader's ultimate goal is to lead or drive the group to the correct destination with God saying, "Good job, faithful servant; you have arrived; you have finished my agenda."

The significance of this last characteristic of navigation attribute can be better understood in the context of Jesus' navigation of the work of salvation. His last statement on the cross before He died was this: "Jesus, knowing that all things were now accomplished, that the Scripture might be fulfilled…He said, "It is finished!" And bowing His head, He gave up His spirit" (John 19:28-30, NKJV). To the Father and to all who could hear His voice then and now, these words mean: "The mission the Father sent Me is accomplished" "It is perfectly completed"; "Father's plan of salvation for humanity is today fulfilled for eternity." In the context of the navigation attribute, it is finished because He was completely submissive and obedient unto death to the course of action mapped out by the Father; He was focused to accomplish that plan, no matter the sacrifice. Hence, salvation is paid in full because of that sacrifice. We hear a similar word from the Apostle Paul: "I have fought the good fight. I have finished the race; I have kept the faith. Henceforth, it is laid up for me a crown of righteousness" (II Timothy 4:7, NKJV). Paul in these scriptures felt that he submitted to God's agenda and had also a sense of satisfaction that he had done God's work in his life.

As a leader-servant, the effectiveness of your navigation attribute is measured by how well you finish the mission God purposes for you; it also means having a sense that you have accomplished the mission. Jesus knew when it was finished (John 19:28a). The Apostle Paul also knew that he had finished the race. The destination stage of navigation requires the leader to have the attitude to finish the mission. The personal leadership attitude is what takes the leader to that finish line. Although preparing, planning and focusing does not guarantee completion, even if the tasks are done correctly, a leader must add perseverance, resilience, self-will, and determination to complete the mission. Here are a few strategies to consider:

Maintain spiritual resilience toward the mission

Spiritual resiliency is the capacity to exercise one's faith, beliefs, and security to build the needed strength and courage to overcome life's challenges. Spiritual resilience empowers people to bounce back from adversities, setbacks, disappointments, discouragements, or hardships. A persistently resilient leader holds firm to a strong belief that "All things work together for good to them that love God and are called according to His purpose" (Romans 8:28, NKJV). This overcoming attitude gives an enduring power of survival to these believers because they always expect to bounce back with God's providence regardless of the situation. They know God is in control and is greater than the situation. In spiritual resilience, the believer sees the finite problem from the perspective of an infinite God.

Nehemiah maintained incredible persistent in the presence of so many odds against completing the task. His persistence was driven by his commitment to finishing. And, he completed it in a record time to the amazement of his enemies and the distracters. As he said, "When all our enemies heard about this, all the surrounding nations were afraid and lost their self-confidence because they realized that this work had been done with the help of our God" (Nehemiah 6:16, NIV).

There are several examples of spiritual resilience in the Bible, and most of the examples depend on a spiritual connection and persistent walk with God. The result is that the leader always bounces back in the presence of challenges, with personal fear turning into strength and imagination. For example, the wilderness experiences turn into a season of growth and greatness. Nehemiah remained focused and was spiritually determined to finish rebuilding. His spiritual resilience turned to fear and opposition into positive strength and focus on finishing well and ahead of schedule.

We can also see other examples of resilience in leaders following their calling or walking with God. Paul showed spiritual resilience and persistence in his missionary work. When the Lord spoke to him, 'For

CHAPTER 6
DEVELOPING EMPATHY–COMPASSION

I am with you, and no one is going to attack and harm you, because I have many people in this city" (Acts 18:10, NIV). Paul showed resilience, bouncing back from a paralyzing fear with strength. The Bible declares he "Stayed for a year and a half in Corinth, teaching them the word of God" (Acts 18:11, NIV). On another occasion, the apostle said, "Now, compelled by the spirit, I am going to Jerusalem, not knowing what will happen to me there (...) However, I consider my life worth nothing to me, if only I may finish the race and complete the task the Lord Jesus has given me - the task of testifying to the gospel of God's grace" (Acts 20:22-24). We see his strong faith, security, and commitment to complete the task, despite of impending suffering.

Job is well-known in Biblical accounts as a man who endured one of the most challenging wilderness experiences recorded. The job was "blameless and upright; he feared God and shunned evil" (Job 1:1, NIV). One would not expect God to allow the devil to bring so much pain and calamity to Job. But through it, all, did Job remain focused? In the end, Job showed resilience after experiencing great hardships by saying, "I know you can do all things; no purpose of yours can be thwarted" (Job 42:2, NIV). We know that job bounced back, and his calamities were turned into considerable prosperity for; "The LORD blessed the latter part of Job's life more than the former part" (Job 42:12, NIV).

Joseph stands alone in his own special wilderness experiences on several dark and difficult fronts. He faced many temptations and adversities, but each time he had a way of bouncing back to a greater level. The Bible says, "But the Lord was with Joseph and showed him mercy, and He gave him favor in the sight of the keeper of the prison" (Genesis 39:21, NKJV). Joseph's strong connection and in his word to his brothers, he said, "And God sent me before you to preserve a posterity for you in the earth, and to save your lives by a great deliverance. So now it was not you who sent me here, but God; and He has made me a father to Pharaoh, and lord of all his house, and a ruler throughout all the land of Egypt" (Genesis 45: 7-9, NKJV). Here, he showed he was a man who bounced back to greatness because he was focused on not sinning against God.

Timothy's wilderness experience was the pressure within and without when the elders looked down on his youthfulness. This story is a particularly good example of today's generation and the peer pressure some of our youth experience. In the words of Paul to Timothy, "Do not let anyone look down on you because you are young. Be in speech, conduct, love, faith, and purity; show yourself to be an example to the believers" (I Timothy 4:12). Timothy showed spiritual resilience. He turned the pressure within and recovered not by talking the talk but by walking the walk of serving by example. In the end, he became a minister of great influence, even to the leaders. He was a young man who "Washed his hands well and hence dined with elders" as an African proverb states.

The wilderness experience of Nelson Mandela precipitated hope for black South Africans. From his prison cell, came great imagination and a determination to stay alive to see the change beyond the walls. He expressed it this way: [12]

> "It is from these comrades in the struggle that I learned the meaning of courage. Time and again, I have seen men and women risk and give their lives for an idea. I have seen men stand up to attack and torture without breaking, showing a strength and resiliency that defy the imagination. I learned that courage was not the absence of fear, but the triumph over it. I felt fear myself more times than I can remember, but I hid it behind a mask of boldness. The brave man is not he who does not feel afraid, but he who conquers that fear."[12]

Mr. Mandela bounced back from his adversities. Spiritual resilience gives leaders the strength to finish strong.

Consider resilience as the power to succeed

I had a course of action to navigate through my doctoral graduate program successfully. But I would not have been successful without the spiritual resilience that gave me an alternative direction at one point in my life. That point was in the fall of 1981. My aspiration for a Ph.D. in a particular engineering department came to a halt. A mere question to clear my confusion in class was interpreted as a challenge to a professor who felt insulted by my query. This simple encounter precipitated hatred and vindictiveness that eventually contributed to the termination of my graduate program in that department. With the letter in my hand, I remember lying down in the middle of a field in a hot summer as if I lost all hope. However, I did not feel defeated. I

CHAPTER 6
DEVELOPING EMPATHY–COMPASSION

was confused but not blinded, discouraged, and at the same time very angry. Naturally, one would ask questions such as "Why me? Where did I go wrong?" And then there was that still voice that said, "This will work together for your good."

Nevertheless, I did not know how. I had always believed that the memory of the past can create aspirations for improving or failing depending on one's perspective. These thoughts and my faith started to instill in my courage. If I allowed this experience to define me, and I accepted that definition, then I would have failed. Even so, if I allowed it to be a season of learning, then I could find another road map to my destiny by repositioning myself. I decided that I must not dwell on that experience, but instead, let it inspire me. How will this happen? I wondered." I still did not know how.

I encouraged myself with another principle; I taught my children: "A failure is only an option if you let it be one." I chose not to let failure be an option. I refused to define it as a failure but instead accepted the experience. I stood up from the field, cleaned up my face, and left the ashes of my anger behind. I went home to share the depression with my lovely wife and a Christian brother who was living with us. After we had all prayed, this brother asked, "Brother Sylvanus, what is another possible roadmap to engineering at this university?" It was a revelation that turned another vision into another path. After earning an MS in Industrial and Applied Physics with a concentration in Geophysics, I applied and went back to the same university to complete a Ph.D. in Engineering Physics, with a double concentration in Nuclear Medical Physics and Petroleum Geology. I became the first person in the university to complete such a rigorous program with no appreciable loss of time in spite of what was supposed to be a setback. I not only bounced back; I gained more. This was resilience.

Navigate abundant spiritual life in Christ.

The beginning point of a great leader-servant is growth in knowledge of Christ, bearing fruit, and helping others bear fruit. A close relationship with Christ and following His teachings and the direction of the Holy Spirit equips us to be great leaders who bear fruit. Such a relationship depends on deep knowledge of Christ and abundant life in Christ. Jesus came to give those who believe in Him not only life but abundant life. "The thief comes only to steal and kill and destroy; I have come that they may have life, and have it more abundantly" (John 10:10, NJKV)

Abundant life is a spirit-filled life that bears and reproduces Christ-like fruit in a born-again believer. Living an abundant life requires our capacity to navigate through a life of freedom, hope, growth, and power, which then enables us to bear different kinds of fruit, including, loving others (John 15:1-15), serving others, developing other leaders, winning souls to Christ and helping them grow (Romans 1:13), sharing with those in need (Romans 15:28), developing a Christ-like character (2 Peter 1:5-8; Galatians 5:22-23), and praising God and giving thanks (Hebrews 13:15).

SUMMARY 6
DEVELOPING NAVIGATION FOR ARRIVAL

Before starting this exercise, please read and follow the instruction in the preface of this workbook. Answers to these questions are contained in this chapter. Completion of these exercises after reading the chapter should take 60-90 minutes.

Discovering the Acts of Navigation-Arrival

1. The leader's ultimate goal is to lead or drive the group to the correct destination with God saying, "Good job, faithful servant; you have arrived; you have finished my agenda."
   a. What is the significance of this last stage of navigation?
   b. How can this be related to Jesus statement, "It is finished!" (John 19:28-30, NKJV). Apostle Paul: "I have fought the good fight. I have finished the race…" (II Timothy 4:7, NKJV)?.
2. How can the effectiveness of your navigation attribute be measured?

Practicing the Acts of Navigation-Arrival

1. **Navigation-destination arrival** stage requires the leader to have the attitude to complete the mission.
   a. What are some strategies a leader can use to make sure he reaches the destination?

CHAPTER 6
DEVELOPING EMPATHY–COMPASSION

    b. How can you or your followers navigate abundant spiritual life in Christ
2. How can a leader add perseverance, resilience, self-will, and deterination to complete the mission? (See (Romans 8:28,; (Nehemiah 6:16; Acts 18:11; Acts 20:22-2; Job 1:1, Job 42:2, 12,; (Genesis 39:21; Genesis 45: 7-9).
3. How do we Navigate abundant spiritual life in Christ? *See* John 10:10; (John 15:1-15; (Romans 1:13; (2 Peter 1:5-8; (Galatians 5:22-23), Hebrews 13:15).
4. With reference to navigation leadership attribute, what take-away, meaning or lesson can you frame to improve your acts of navigation-arrival (finishing) in a leadership process?
5. Write a commitment statement for plan to improve

TOPIC INDEX

About This Book, 22
Affective Compassion, 63
authentic, 24, 26
authentic leadership, 37
Authentic Leadership, 45
Authenticity, 43
Comfort, 41
commitment, 19, 25, 57, 65, 70, 71
communication
  types of, 30
Communication, 30
Comparisons
  with other works, 40
Compassion, 28
credibility, 48
Empathy-attribute, 28
expectations, 51
focus, 59
  navigation, 66
Functional Definitions, 35
giving, 57, 74
Initiative
  definition of, 29
inside-out, 46
Joshua, 19, 61, 62
law of, 42
LEADER, 28
Leader as Servant Leadership, 42
  definition, 25
Leader First., 23
Leader-as-Servant Leadership, 23
leader-servant's affection-attribute
  definition, 48
leadership, 25
Leadership Attributes, 43
Leadership Inner Value system, 25
Model, 23
Moses, 19
Mr. Mandella, 72
Navigating Abundant, 73, 75
Navigation
  Focusing On Details, 66
Navigation Chart
  Align action with purpose, 61, 62
  Be prepared for sacrifice in the work, 57
Navigation Focus
  Be decisive of on your direction, 59, 66
  Be decisive of on your direction, 64

Be decisive of on your direction, 66
Watch out for Distracters, 59, 66
Watch out for Distracters, 64
Watch out for Distracters, 66
Watch the Front and back of the mission, 65
Navigation Preparation
  Plan with Correct Information, 55
Navigation Preparation
  Map Course of Action, 56
Navigation Preparation
  Understand the Cultures Involved, 56
Navigation Preparation
  Map Course of Action, 57
Navigation-attribute, 48
Navigation-Chart
  definition, 61, 62
Navigation-focus
  definition, 63, 66
Navigation-preparation
  definition of, 55, 57, 58
ommunication
  culture-based, 56
Personal Outward Authenticity, 47
Practicing Servant Leadership
  Navigation, 58
process, 25
Resilience, 72
Road -Map for Navigation, 58
Servant, 23, 24
spiritual resilience, 70, 72
Spiritual resiliency
  definition, 70
suffering, 71
Teachable Moments to Grow, 67
test
  for leader-servant authenticity, 46
  of essential elements of personal
    authenticity, 46, 47
The Leadership Influence-attribute, 41
The Principle of Leadership Empathy-
  Attribute, 28
The Principle of Leadership Adaptability
  Attribute, 27
The Principle of Leadership listening-
  attribute, 30
Timothy, 71
wilderness experience, 71, 72

REFERENCES

[1]Greenleaf, R. (1970). *The Servant as Leader,* Indianapolis: The Robert K. Greenleaf Center

[2]Spears, L. (1996). *"Reflections on Robert K. Greenleaf and servant-leadership."* Leadership & Organization Development Journal, 17(7), 33-35

[3]Russell, R.F. (2001). "The role of values in servant leadership." *Leadership & Organization Development Journal,* 22(2), 76-83

[4]Russell, R.F., and Stone, A.G. (2002). "A review of servant leadership attributes: developing a practical model." *Leadership & Organization Development Journal,* 23(3), 145-15

[5]Terry. R. W (1993). *Authentic Leadership: Courage In Action,* San Francisco, CA, Jossey-Bass

[6]George, B (2003). *Authentic Leadership: Rediscovering the Secrets to Creating Lasting Value.* San Francisco, CA, Jossey-Bass

[7]Shamir, B. & Eilam, G. (2005). "What's your story? Toward a life-story approach to authentic leadership." Leadership Quarterly, 16, 395–418.

[8]Anderson, GL (2009). *Advocacy Leadership: Toward a Post-Reform Agenda in Education,* Routledge, New York, 41

[9]Yacobi, B.G. *"Elements of Human Authenticity."* http://www.philosophytogo.org /wordpress/?p=1945, Retrieved, July 15, 2012

[10]George, B (2003). *Authentic Leadership: Rediscovering the Secrets to Creating Lasting Value,* San Francisco, CA, Jossey-Bass

[11]Wosu, SN (2014), *Leader as Servant Leadership Model,* Xulon Press

[12] Mandela, Nelson, *Long Walk to Freedom,* Little Brown and Company, New York. 22[13]http://en.wikipedia.org/wiki/Sympathy

[13]Stengel, Richard (2008), "Mandela: His 8 Lessons of Leadership", *Time,* July 21 p. 42-49,

[14]KnowledgeWorkx's Cultural Mapping & Navigation (CMN) Certification Workshop. https://www.knowledgeworkx.com

[15] Maxwell, J.C. *21 Irrefutable Laws of Leadership: Follow them and People will Follow you*, Nelson Business, P. 42.